JURASSIC STRIKE FORCE 5

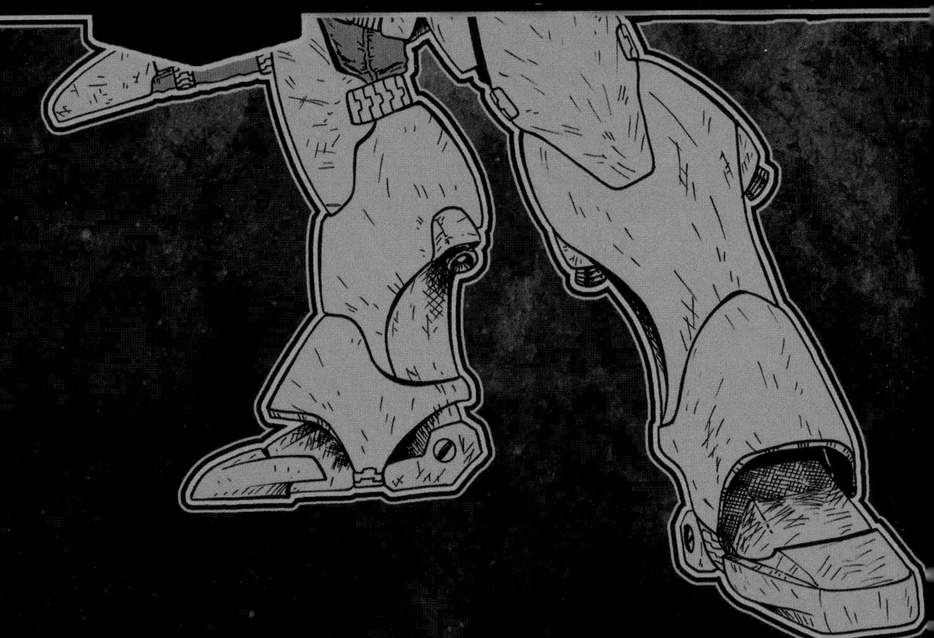

THIS VOLUME REPRINTS THE COMIC SERIES JURASSIC STRIKE FORCE 5, ISSUES #0-5 PUBLISHED BY SILVER DRAGON BOOKS. SECOND EDITION, DECEMBER, 2014 • ISBN: 978-1-942275-03-9

Jurassic Strike Force 5 Trade Paperback, December, 2014. Second Printing. Published by Silver Dragon Books Inc. an imprint of Zenescope Entertainment Inc., 433 Caredean Drive, Ste. C, Horsham, Pennsylvania 19044.

Prelude
WRITER JOE BRUSHA ART JULIAN AGUILERA
COLORS THOMAS MASON LETTERS ARTMONKEYS

FOR OVER 165 MILLION YEARS DINOSAURS RULED OUR PLANET.

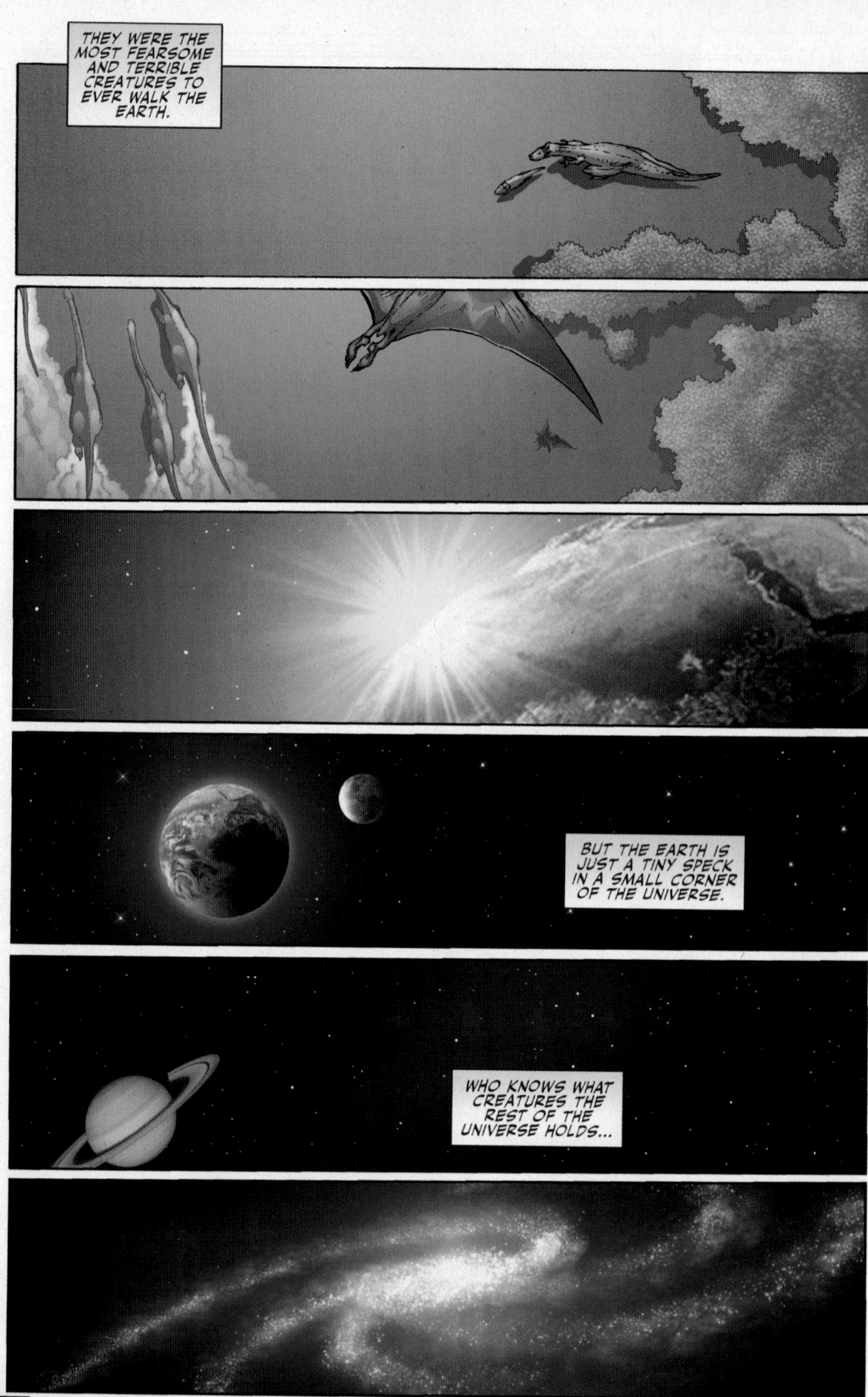
THEY WERE THE MOST FEARSOME AND TERRIBLE CREATURES TO EVER WALK THE EARTH.
BUT THE EARTH IS JUST A TINY SPECK IN A SMALL CORNER OF THE UNIVERSE.
WHO KNOWS WHAT CREATURES THE REST OF THE UNIVERSE HOLDS...

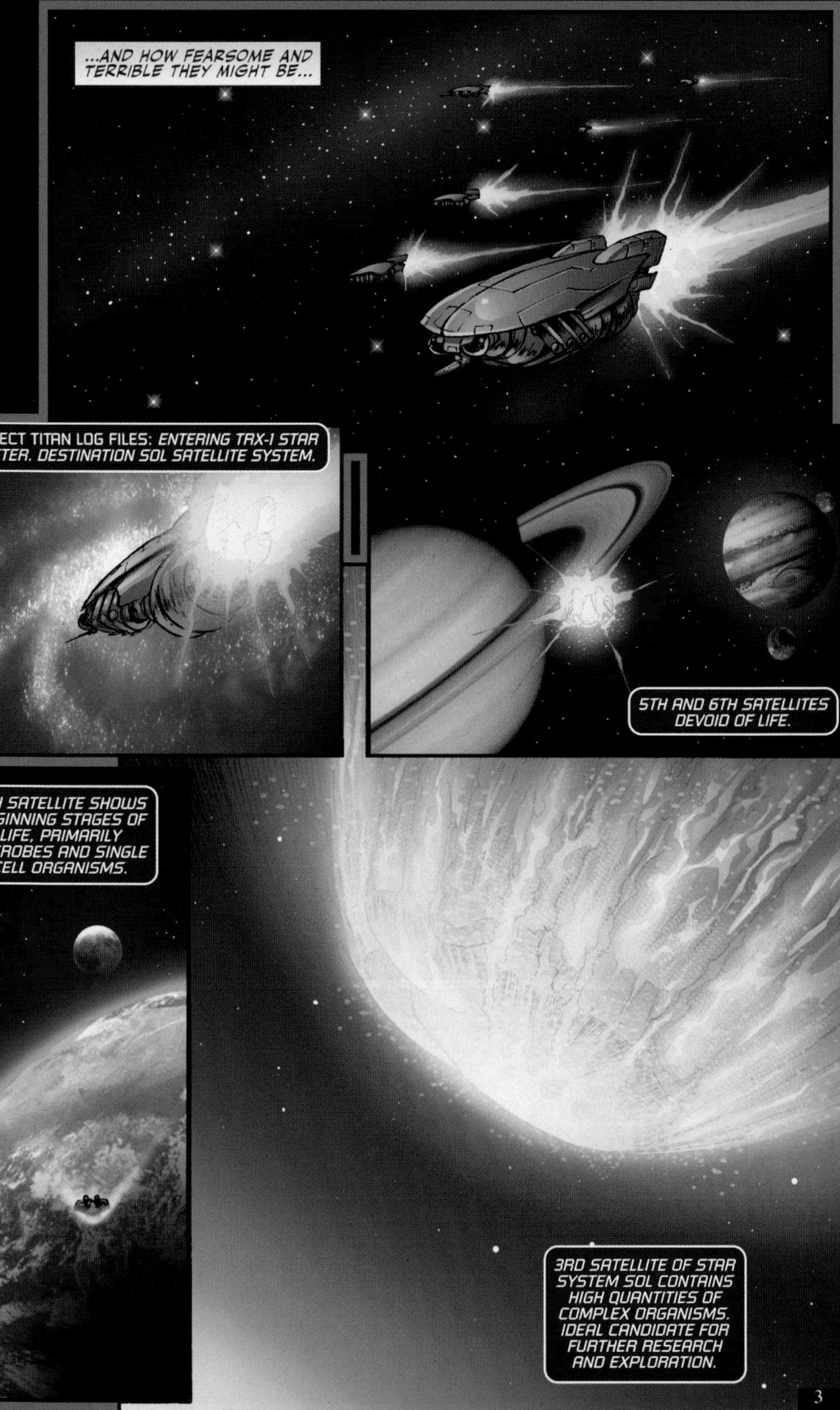
...AND HOW FEARSOME AND TERRIBLE THEY MIGHT BE...
PROJECT TITAN LOG FILES: ENTERING TRX-1 STAR CLUSTER. DESTINATION SOL SATELLITE SYSTEM.
5TH AND 6TH SATELLITES DEVOID OF LIFE.
4TH SATELLITE SHOWS BEGINNING STAGES OF LIFE, PRIMARILY MICROBES AND SINGLE CELL ORGANISMS.
3RD SATELLITE OF STAR SYSTEM SOL CONTAINS HIGH QUANTITIES OF COMPLEX ORGANISMS. IDEAL CANDIDATE FOR FURTHER RESEARCH AND EXPLORATION.

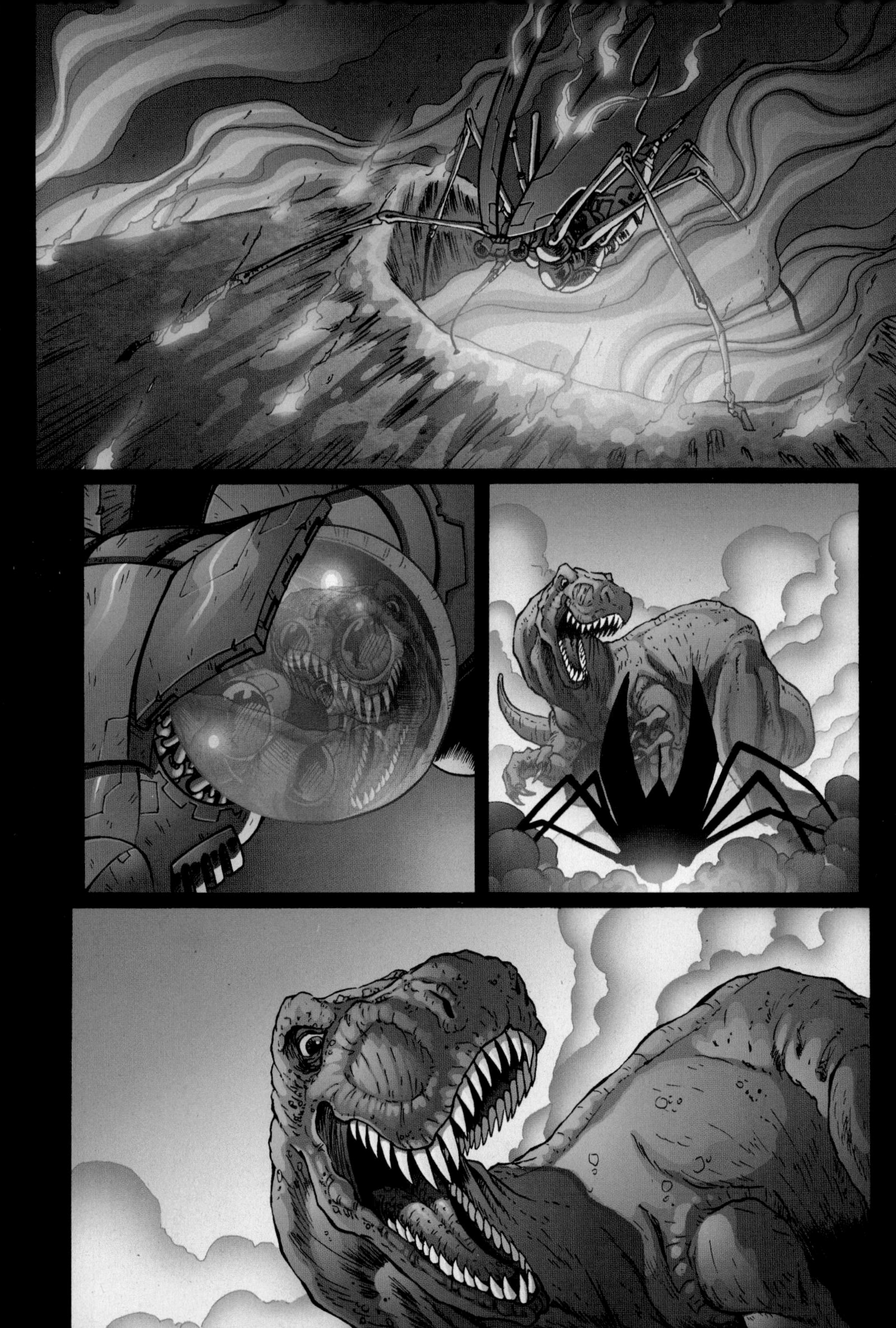

RUN GENETIC MUTATION SEQUENCING PROGRAM.

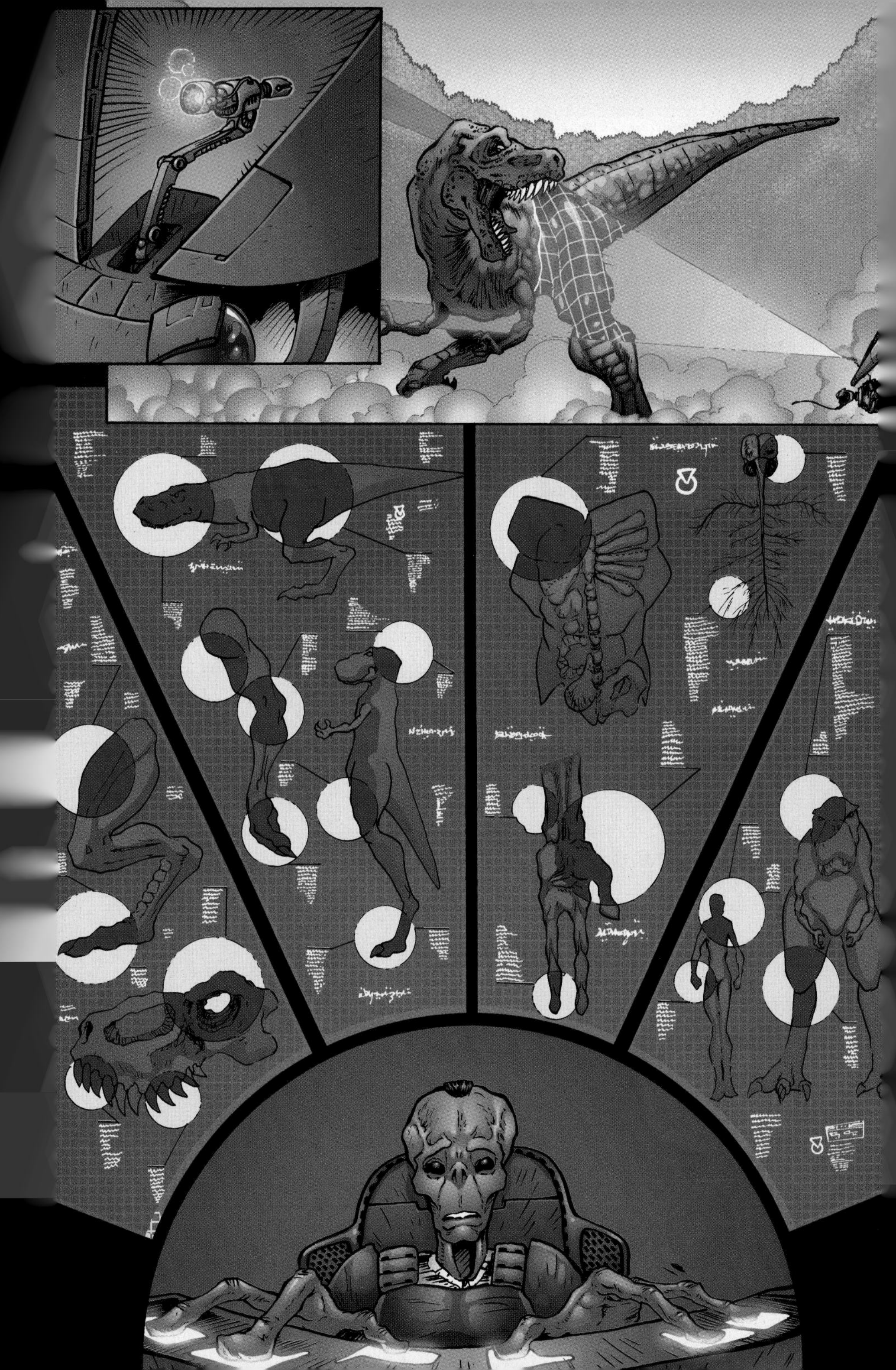

PROBE DROID TITAN 74567
PROBE DROID TITAN 74567
SET COORDINATES FOR THE THIRD SATELLITE OF THE SOL SYSTEM.

JURASSIC STRIKE FORCE 5

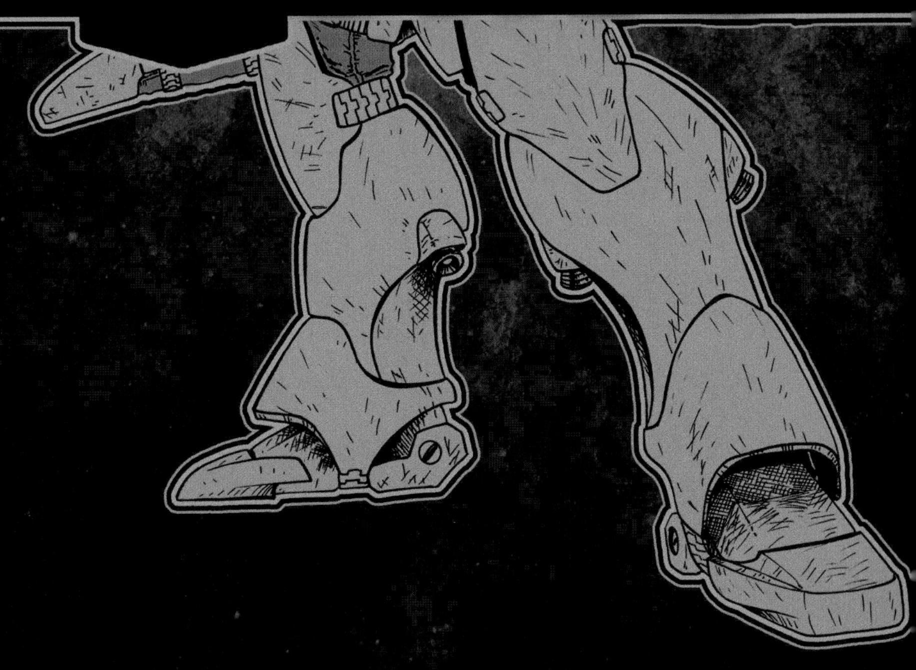

Chapter One

WRITER NEO EDMUND ART JL GILES-RIVERA
COLORS JEFF BALKE LETTERS JIM CAMPBELL

ANTARCTICA,
EXCAVATION SITE
ALPHA --

I'VE NEVER SEEN MARKINGS LIKE THIS, SIR. WHO COULD HAVE MADE THEM?
WHO? OR WHAT?
LET'S GET THE THERMAL CUTTER DOWN THERE.

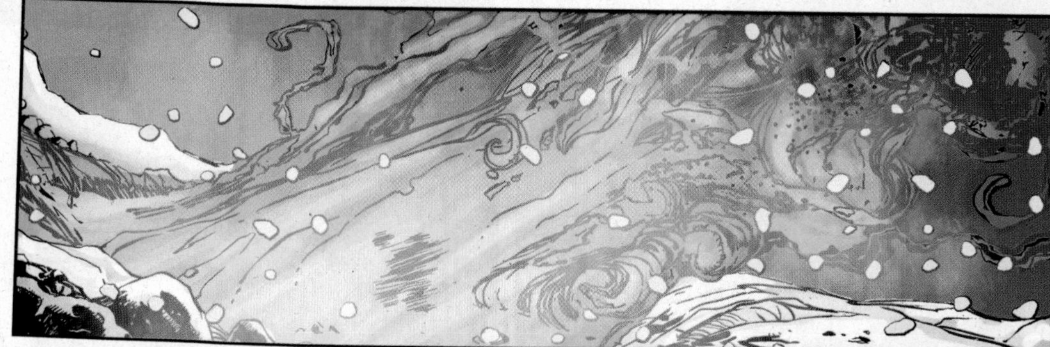

AFTER 160 MILLION YEARS OF IMPRISONMENT, I AM FREE.
AND VENGEANCE WILL BE MINE.

I'M PICKING UP ELECTRICAL ACTIVITY.
IMPOSSIBLE. THIS THING HAS BEEN BURIED FOR CENTURIES.

THIS MATERIAL IS STRONGER THAN ANY I'VE EVER SEEN. CRANK UP THE JUICE.
WE'RE ALREADY RUNNING AT MAXIMUM POWER.

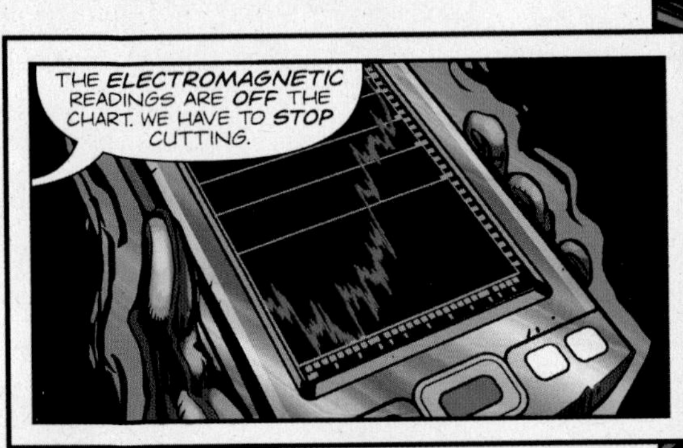
THE ELECTROMAGNETIC READINGS ARE OFF THE CHART. WE HAVE TO STOP CUTTING.

WE'VE GOT A SERIOUS PROBLEM!
GET OUT OF HERE.
QUICK!
RUMMMMMMMMMMMBLE

MOVE FASTER. IT'S GOING TO BLOW!
IT'S THE MOST AMAZING THING I'VE EVER SEEN.
GET OUT OF THERE, YOU IDIOT!

ZHMMMMMMM

FZAAKK

WHERE DO I FIND THE RULERS OF THIS WORLD? TELL ME NOW, WORM!
WHAAAA--?
WASHINGTON DC, I GUESS.

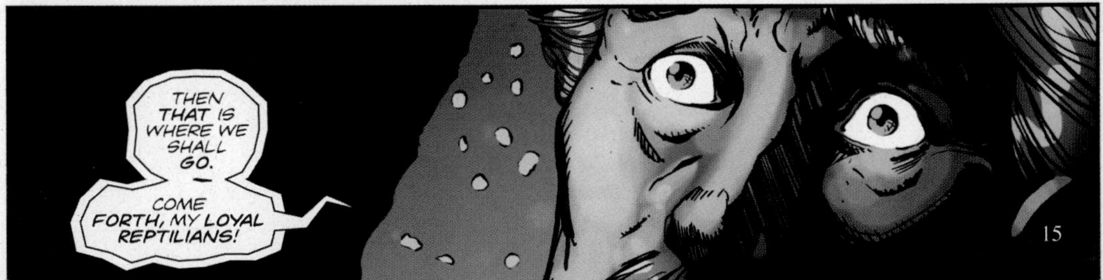
THEN THAT IS WHERE WE SHALL GO.
COME FORTH, MY LOYAL REPTILIANS!

OUR TIME TO RULE THE GALAXY HAS COME.

RESEARCH EXCAVATION SITE DELTA--

10 MILES NORTH OF SITE ALPHA.

WHOA! MAJOR DISASTER!

DAD!

YOU GOTTA SEE THIS!

DAD?
THIS PLACE IS MESSIER THAN MY ROOM.
WHOA, WAIT A MINUTE...
...MOST DEFINITELY ALIENS!
YIKES!
PANIC TIME!
EASY NOW! I COME IN PEACE. SURE HOPE YOU DO!
NO FACIAL RECOGNITION. ELIMINATE SECURITY THREAT!

WHOA! BAD FORM! DIDN'T YOU READ THE MANUAL ON INTERGALACTIC DIPLOMACY?

REPEAT AFTER ME -- THE FREAKED OUT HUMAN IS A FRIEND.
CAN YOU SAY FRIEND?

TRANSLATING:
FRIEND = FAVORED COMPANION

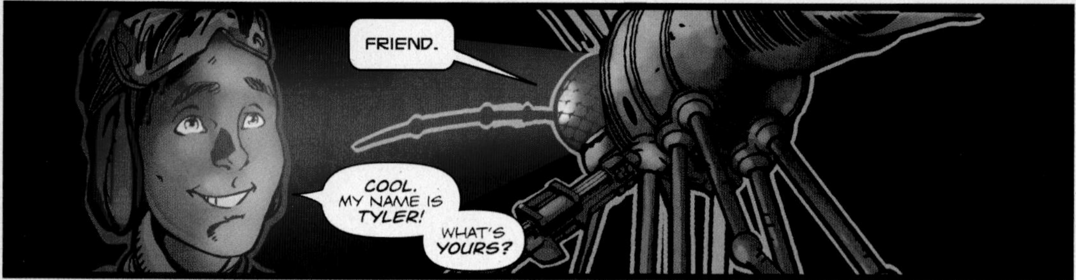
FRIEND.
COOL. MY NAME IS TYLER!
WHAT'S YOURS?

BUZZZZZZ BUZZZZZZ
SOUNDS LIKE SOME KIND OF ALARM. I SURE HOPE DAD'S OKAY!

COME BACK! WE WERE JUST STARTING TO GET SOMEWHERE.

WAIT UP!
THIS BUG IS SUPER FAST!

WAIT UP, BUG. I ALREADY MADE FIRST CONTACT!

PLEASE! WE MEAN NO HARM!

HOLD UP, BUG FACE! THAT'S MY DAD!

TYLER, WHAT ARE YOU DOING HERE?

DON'T WORRY, DAD! WE'RE ALL FRIENDS.

REMEMBER, BUG FACE? FRIENDS!

FRIEND!

REMARKABLE!

BUZZZZZ BUZZZZZ

NOT ANOTHER ALARM. NOW WHAT?

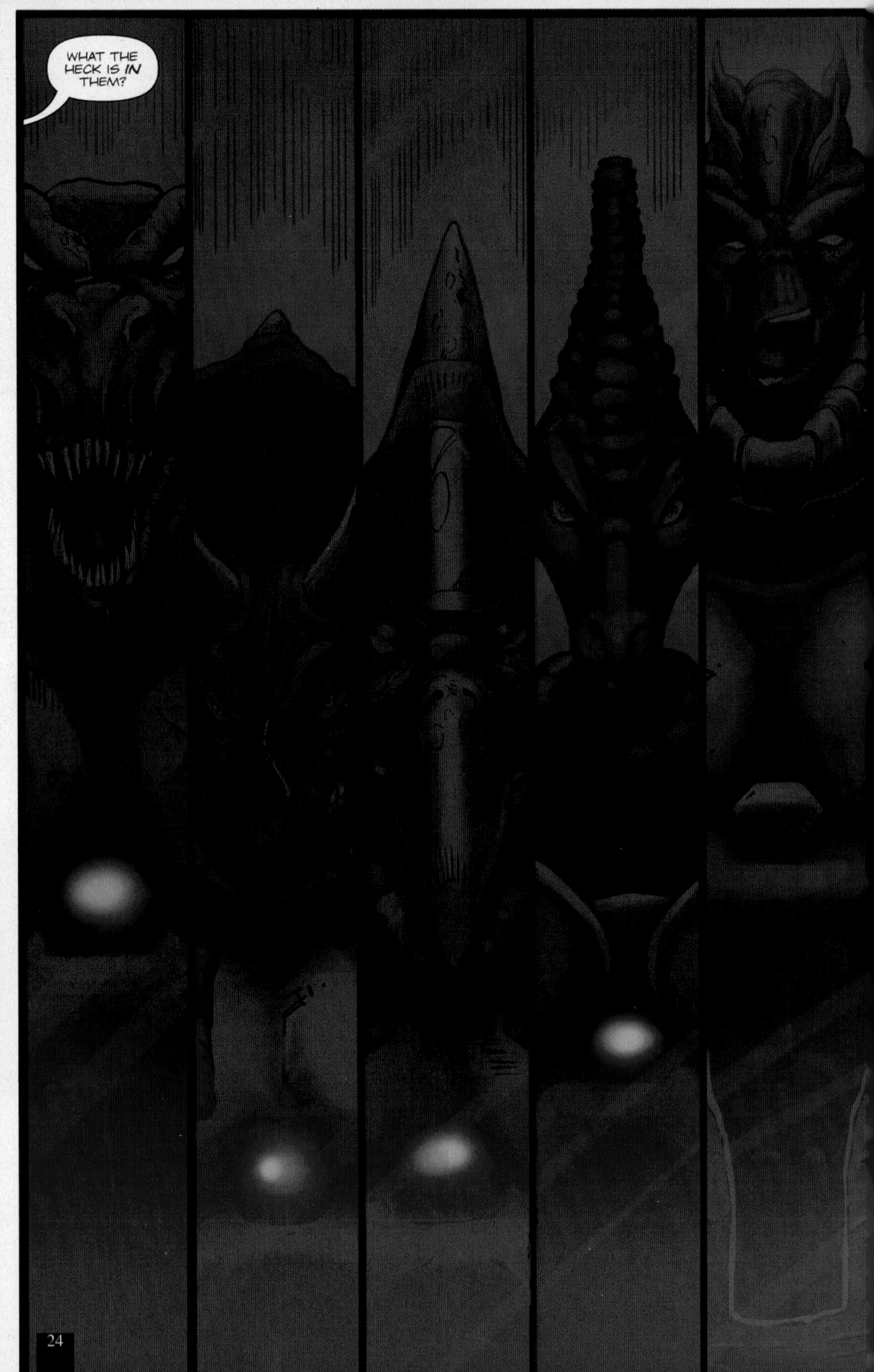
WHAT THE HECK IS *IN* THEM?

U.S. SUBMARINE BASE -- ANTARCTICA.

100 MILES SOUTH OF EXCAVATION SITE DELTA.

GENERAL, I HAVE AN ***UNIDENTIFIED OBJECT*** ON APPROACH FROM THE ***NORTH,*** TRAVELING AT AN ***EXTREME*** RATE OF SPEED.

REPTILIANS! ATTACK!
AROOOGA AROOOGA

SURRENDER OR YOU WILL BE DESTROYED!

FIRE!

BRAKKA BRAKKA

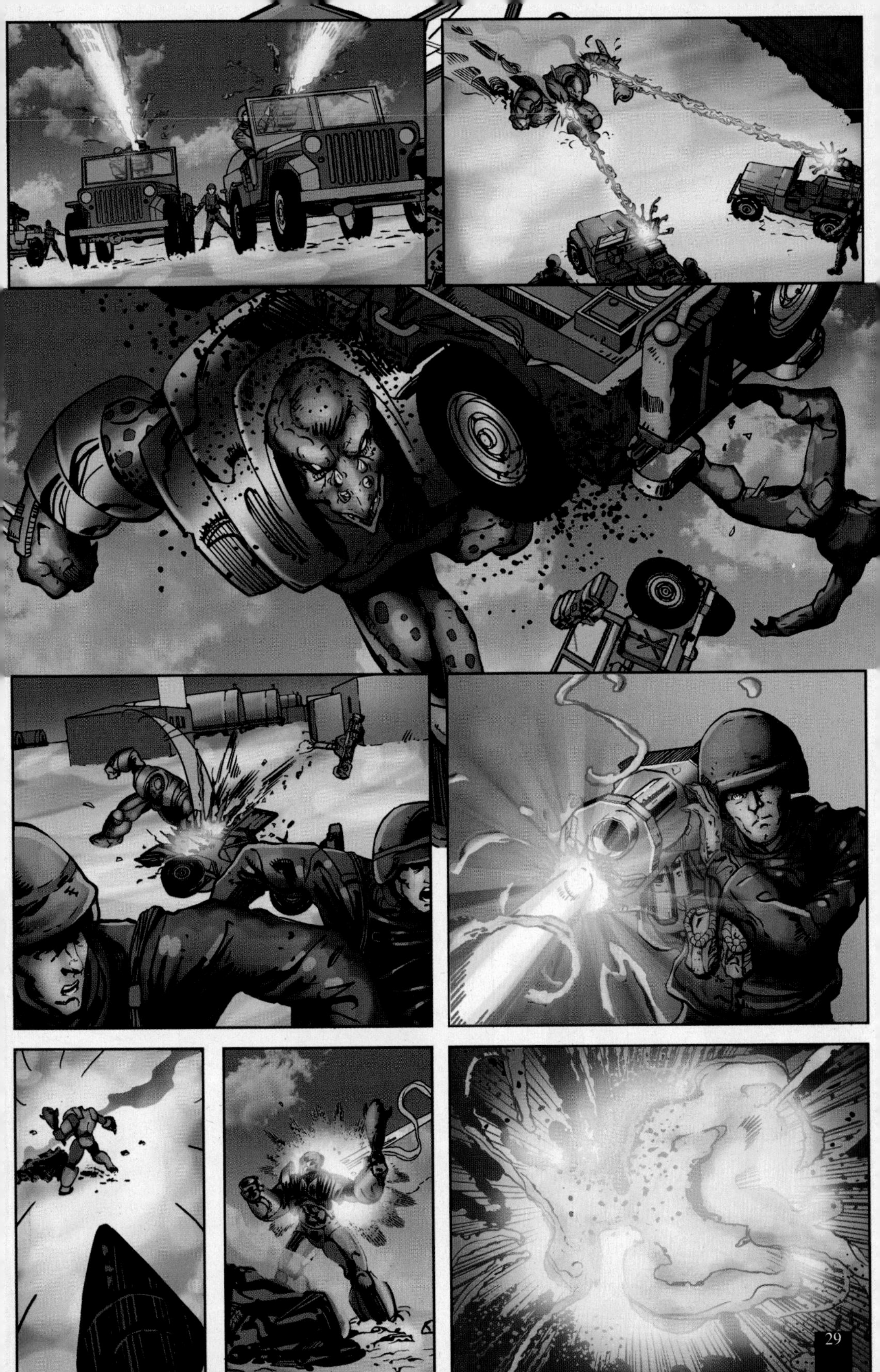

WE WILL NOT BE DEFEATED WITH SUCH **FUTILE** WEAPONS, YOU **FOOLISH** HUMAN.

YOU DARE CHALLENGE **ME!**

FOOM
WE ARE INVINCIBLE! WHO ELSE DARES TO CHALLENGE OUR SUPERIORITY?

ENOUGH! MEN, LOWER YOUR WEAPONS!

I DON'T KNOW WHO OR WHAT YOU ARE, BUT I KNOW WHEN WE'RE BEATEN.
IF YOU'LL SPARE MY MEN, I WILL SURRENDER!

YOU ARE SMARTER THAN YOU APPEAR, MAGGOT! VICTORY IS OURS!

IF YOU VALUE THE LIVES OF YOUR MEN YOU WILL TELL ME WHERE YOUR NUCLEAR WARHEADS ARE STORED.

NO ONE CAN DEFEAT MY REPTILIAN WARRIORS. WE ARE UNSTOPPABLE!
EARTH WILL SOON KNOW THE POWER OF ZALEX... THEN THE GALAXY WILL BE MINE TO RULE AS IT WAS 160 MILLION YEARS AGO.
WHOA...

RRRAAAAWWWWRRR

ZALEX AND HIS REPTILIANS MUST BE BACK. AND THAT MEANS WE'VE GOT BIG TROUBLE.
I'M INTERCEPTING AN ENCRYPTED TRANSMISSION. SHOULD BE EASY ENOUGH TO DECODE.
IT'S A DISTRESS SIGNAL. A MILITARY BASE IS UNDER ATTACK BY AN UNKNOWN ENEMY.
IT MUST BE THE SUBMARINE BASE. THAT COMPLEX HOUSES NUCLEAR WEAPONS.
THAT SOUNDS LIKE A MAJOR CRISIS!

AM I THE ONLY ONE WONDERING WHAT EXACTLY THESE CREATURES ARE?
HEY! PUT ME DOWN, DRAGON BREATH.
SPIKE, LEAVE HIM BE. WE KNOW NOTHING OF THIS WORLD. IF WE'RE GOING TO STOP ZALEX, WE NEED THEIR HELP.

STRIKEFORCE, GEAR UP! IT'S TIME FOR ACTION!

I LIKE THE SOUND OF THAT.

Chapter Two
WRITER NEO EDMUND ART JL GILES-RIVERA
COLORS JEFF BALKE LETTERS JIM CAMPBELL

ANTARCTICA, EXCAVATION SITE DELTA--

IT'S BEEN EIGHT HOURS SINCE WE'VE HAD CONTACT WITH TYLER AND DOCTOR CONNOR.
WE BETTER ORGANIZE A SEARCH PARTY.
RUMMMMMMMBBBBBLE

AVALANCHE! RUN FOR YOUR LIFE!

100 MILLION YEARS *DORMANT* AND THE *STRIKE-TANK* IS STILL READY TO KICK SOME *REPTILIAN TAIL*.
NOBODY BUILDS 'EM LIKE *YOU* DO, TANK!
A *REMARKABLE* FEAT OF ENGINEERING.
THIS THING *SO* ROCKS!

ARE WE *THERE* YET?

FORGET TO GO TO THE *LITTLE DINOSAUR'S* ROOM BEFORE WE LEFT THE HOUSE, SPIKE?
ETA TO THE *SUBMARINE BASE*. FOURTEEN MINUTES.

LISTEN UP, STRIKE FORCE. DO NOT TAKE *ANY* ACTION THAT PUTS THE *HUMANS* AT *RISK*.

THE *REPTILIANS* WON'T BE AS *CAREFUL*, SO KEEP YOUR HEADS *LOW* IF YOU DON'T WANNA *LOSE* 'EM.

U.S. SUBMARINE BASE, ANTARCTICA--

KRANNG

THE HUMANS WERE **DIFFICULT** TO **CONTROL** AT FIRST, BUT THEY ARE NOW FOLLOWING OUR **ORDERS** WITHOUT CONFLICT.
EXCELLENT. WE WILL MAKE EVERY LAST ONE OF THEM OUR **MINIONS** NOW THAT THE **NODES** ARE **EXTINCT.**

TAKE **EVERY** SCRAP OF **METAL**. WE'LL NEED IT TO BUILD OUR **ULTIMATE WEAPON.**
WE WILL **CONQUER THIS** WORLD, THEN THE **GALAXY!**

OUTTA MY WAY, BEAK FACE! I GOTTA GET THIS LOADED UP.
THE CARGO HOLD IS FULL. SAVE IT FOR THE NEXT TRIP.
I AIN'T TAKIN' NO BOSSING FROM A WINGED GIRLY.
YOU WON'T BE SAYING THAT WHEN MASTER ZALEX PUTS ME IN COMMAND.
I SAYS WE FINISH THIS HERES AND NOWS!
SHOW ME WHAT YOU GOT, ROCK BRAIN!
BDAM
BDAM
BDAM
FWAM
WHUD

NOW I FINISH YOUS, GIRLY GIRL.
TAKE YOUR BEST SHOT.
SHRAAK
ENOUGH OF THIS FOOLISHNESS! BACK TO WORK BEFORE I FINISH BOTH OF YOU.
PERMANENTLY!
LET'S SAY WE CALL IT A DRAW, ROCK BRAINS.
I CAN LIVES WITH THAT FOR NOW, GIRLY GIRL.
MASTER ZALEX.
WE HAVE URGENT NEWS.
THERE'S VERY LITTLE TIME.
FOES ARE APPROACHING FROM THE SOUTH!
REPTILIANS, PREPARE FOR BATTLE!

WE'RE WAITIN' FOR YA, STRIKE FORCE.
BRING IT ON!
STRIKE FORCE, PREPARE FOR ACTION.
AH-YEAH. HERE WE GO!
BRACE FOR IMPACT!

THWAAM

REPTILIANS, ONE!
STRIKE-TANK, SCRAP METAL!!
LET US FINISH THEM.
ANNIHILATE!
BDAM
BLAM
BLAM
KBLAM
BDAM
DIE, STRIKE FORCE!

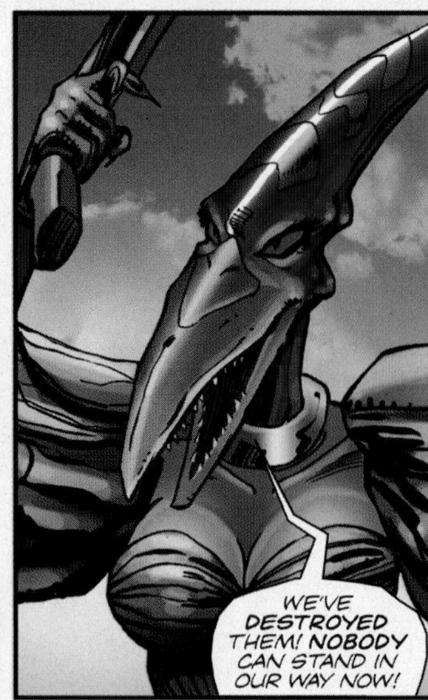
WE'VE DESTROYED THEM! NOBODY CAN STAND IN OUR WAY NOW!

LET US BE SURE.
RAZOR AND TALON. RIP IT OPEN.

IT WILL BE OUR PLEASURE!
REVEAL OUR ENEMY'S FINAL DEMISE, WE SHALL.

STRIFE, INVESTIGATE.

NOT ME. SEND THE ROCK BRAIN INSIDE.

I AIN'T GETTING BLASTED TO BITS IN THERE.

STEP ASIDE, COWARDS. I WILL DETERMINE THEIR FATES ON MY OWN!

A PITY YOU WENT DOWN SO EASILY, MY BROTHER!
ANY CHANCE YOU CAN SAY FRIEND?
PLEASE. WE COME IN PEACE!
PERHAPS YOU DO. BUT I DO NOT!

FAREWELL, STRIKE FORCE.
I DON'T THINK SO, ROCK BRAIN.
CATCH THIS.
NOOOO!
DON'T WORRY. I GOTS IT!
FOOM

STRIKE FORCE, RISE UP!
NOW WE'RE GOING TO SEE SOME SERIOUS ACTION!

REPTILIANS!
LET US MAKE THEM
EXTINCT!

I DON'T WANT TO FIGHT YOU, BROTHER.
THEN YOU WILL BE DESTROYED!
SHRAAKK
KRZZT
THWAK
FWAM
BROTHER, JOIN FORCES WITH ME SO WE CAN DESTROY ZALEX... TOGETHER.
BETRAY MY MASTER? NEVER!

I'LL DESTROY YOU BOTH IN ONE BLAST THEN MASTER ZALEX WILL PUT ME IN COMMAND.
WHOOPS.
DID I DO THAT?
I'LL MAKE YOU REGRET THAT!
IF I DIDN'T KNOW BETTER, I'D THINK YOU WERE TRYING TO HIT ME.
YOU CAN'T EVADE ME FOREVER!
WHO SAYS I WAS TRYING?
SWOOFF
BEST BEHAVE OR I'LL HAVE TO CLIP YOUR WINGS, LITTLE LADY!
CURSE YOU!

IT'S BEEN A LONG TIME, OLD FRIEND.
100 MILLION YEARS WITHOUT SEEING YOUR UGLY MUG AIN'T LONG ENOUGH.

RARRRR!
KTHUD
ARRRRGGGGGH!

HOPE THAT'S NOT THE BEST YOU GOT!
THWAK

I HAVEN'T EVEN GOT STARTED.

FWAM

AND IT LOOKS LIKE YOU'RE MORE THAN FINISHED.

THUD

THWAK

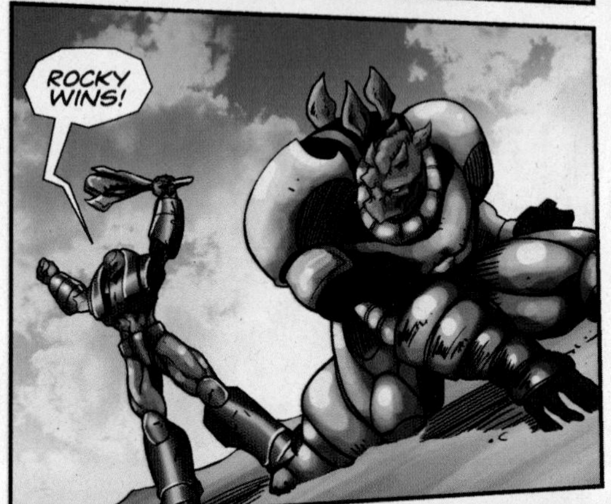
ROCKY WINS!

I'M SUPPOSED TO GET A **TEN COUNT** BEFORE YOU COUNT ME **OUT**, BLOCKHEAD.

FWAK

THOK

FWAM

1... 2... 3...
...10.
YOU'RE OUT!

<PASSCODE REQUIRED>

THERE'S NO SYSTEM THAT CAN KEEP THIS GIRL OUT!

<PASSCODE ACCEPTED>
I AM SOOOO GOOD.
NOW, LET'S SEE WHAT YOU REPTILIANS ARE UP TO.

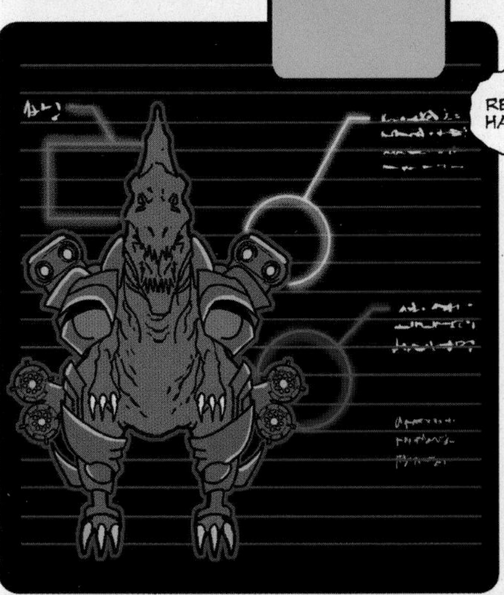

THIS IS REALLY BAD. I HAVE TO WARN REX!

IT SEEMS WE HAVE AN INTRUDER.
SHE MUST BE ELIMINATED.

THAT'S ONE LITTLE PIGGY DOWN.

MAKE THAT TWO.

CALL IT THREE.

YOUR REPTILIANS ARE DEFEATED. SURRENDER OR BE DESTROYED.

WE HAVE NOT EVEN BEGUN TO FIGHT.
LET US FINISH THIS ONCE AND FOR ALL!

RARAHHHH!

SHZAAK

KRZZT

WHUD
THOK

SURRENDER, KANE. DON'T MAKE ME DESTROY YOU.

FOOL. IT IS YOU THAT WILL SURRENDER.

WE WILL NEVER BE DEFEATED. NOW LAY DOWN YOUR WEAPONS...
OR ELSE!
OH, NO! WE GOTTA DO SOMETHING OR THE EARTH IS TOTALLY DOOMED.

JURASSIC STRIKE FORCE 5

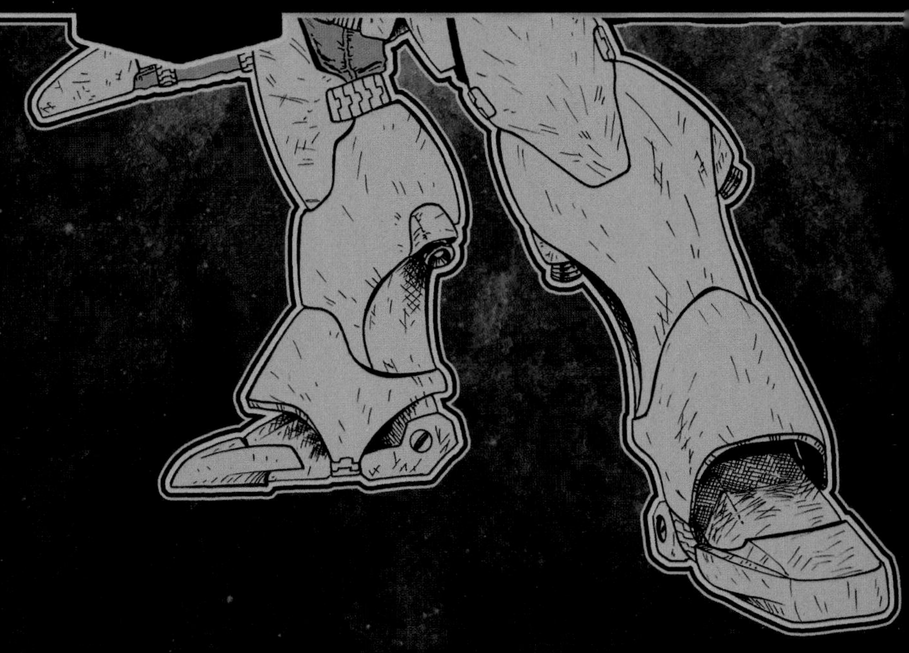

DUALAND
Chapter Three
WRITER NEO EDMUND ART JL GILES-RIVERA
COLORS JEFF BALKE LETTERS JIM CAMPBELL

YOU SHOULD HAVE LET THEM DESTROY ME RATHER THAN SURRENDER.
DON'T WORRY, WE'LL FIND A WAY OUT OF THIS!
SILENCE! DON'T MAKE ME WARN YOU AGAIN!
WHAT'S WITH ALL THE METAL, STRIFE? WHAT ARE YOU REPTILIANS UP TO?
THEY'RE BUILDING SOME KIND OF SUPER WEAPON...
WHAT PART OF SILENCE DID YOU ROCK BRAINS FAIL TO UNDERSTAND?
GET THEM INSIDE! MASTER ZALEX AWAITS THEM.
DAD, WE HAVE TO HELP STRIKE FORCE OR THE WORLD IS TOTALLY DOOMED.

STRUGGLE ALL YOU WANT, YOUR CAGES HAVE BEEN REINFORCED TO ASSURE THERE WILL BE NO ESCAPE.

RAHHHHH!

REX, IT SEEMS YOUR COMPASSION FOR YOUR SOLDIERS HAS LED TO YOUR CAPTURE.

THEY ARE NOT MERELY MY SOLDIERS, KANE. THEY ARE MY FRIENDS.

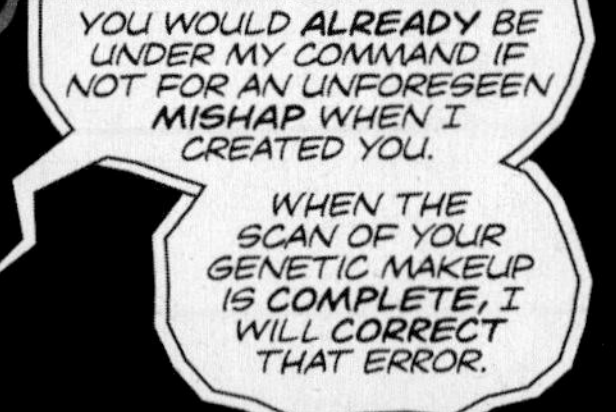

ONCE MASTER ZALEX TURNS STRIKE FORCE TO OUR SIDE THERE WILL BE NOTHING TO STOP US.
IF I WERE IN COMMAND WE WOULD HAVE ALREADY DESTROYED THEM.
Oh, NO! IT'S WORSE THAN WE THOUGHT!
WE NEED A PLAN... QUICK.
DO YOU HAVE ANY IDEAS?
BEEP BEEP BUZZBEEP
COMPUTING RESCUE STRATEGY.
HEY, WHERE YOU GOING?
WE BETTER FOLLOW IT.

<ACCESSING MISSION LOGS>

EARTH MISSION
++ LOG ENTRY 1.0 ++
3RD SATELLITE OF STAR SYSTEM
HIGH QUANTITIES OF COMPLEX ORGANISMS.
IDEAL CANDIDATE FOR RESEARCH AND EXPLORATION
100 MILLION YEARS AGO.
Master, the planet's atmosphere won't support my people's **biology** for long.
IF YOU WRETCHED NODES CANNOT **PROPERLY** SERVE MY NEEDS THEN I WILL JUST **DESTROY** YOU NOW.

Our scans show the life forms are primitive... and extremely **hostile.**
ALL THE BETTER!

INTERESTING.

VERY INTERESTING!

RAWRRRR
HELLO, MY MAGNIFICENT FRIEND!

I THINK YOUR MOTHER HAS COME TO GREET ME!
WHUDD
FWAM
RAWRRRRR
NOW IT IS MY TURN!

THWAM
RAHHHHHH!
THWAAK
FWAM
VICTORY IS MINE!
THUD
YOU WERE A VALIANT FOE, MY FRIEND.
WORTHY OF SERVING AS THE MOLD FOR MY NEW RACE OF GENETICALLY ENHANCED WARRIORS.

YOU SHALL BE MY ULTIMATE WEAPON!

THE NODES' SCIENCE STARSHIP ARRIVES ON EARTH--
THE NODES' GENETIC RESEARCH LABORATORY--
I must protest! Our genetic technology isn't meant to create soldiers for war.
PROCEED AS I COMMAND OR I WILL ORDER THE TOTAL ANNIHILATION OF YOUR ENTIRE WORLD.
You're a monster, Zalex.
THAT'S MASTER ZALEX TO YOU!
YOU WILL PERFORM THE GENETIC MUTATION OF THE EGGS OR TASTE THE COLD STEEL OF MY BLADE.

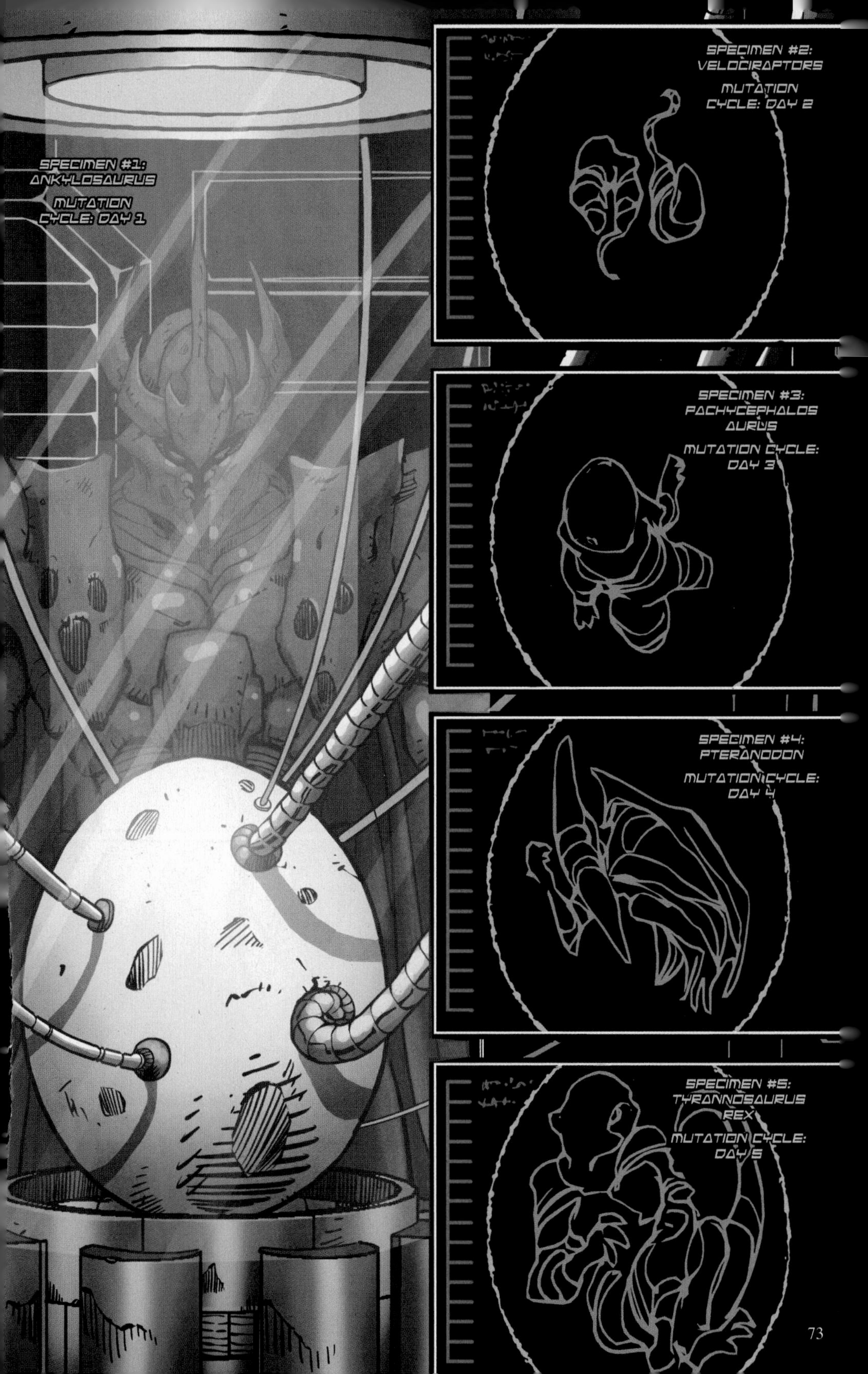
SPECIMEN #1:
ANKYLOSAURUS
MUTATION
CYCLE: DAY 1
SPECIMEN #2:
VELOCIRAPTORS
MUTATION
CYCLE: DAY 2
SPECIMEN #3:
PACHYCEPHALOS
AURUS
MUTATION CYCLE:
DAY 3
SPECIMEN #4:
PTERANODON
MUTATION CYCLE:
DAY 4
SPECIMEN #5:
TYRANNOSAURUS
REX
MUTATION CYCLE:
DAY 5

MUTATION
CYCLE: DAY 6

MUTATION
CYCLE: DAY 7
KRAASH
SKAASH
RISE UP, MY MAGNIFICENT SERVANT!

RAWWRR!
I HAVE DONE IT!

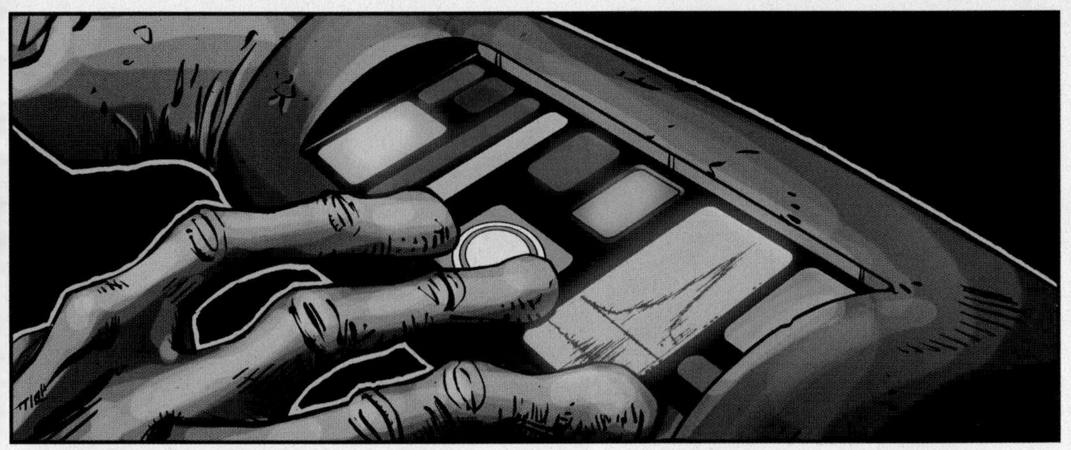

MUTATION CYCLE:
DAY 5

You are the galaxy's **only** hope.

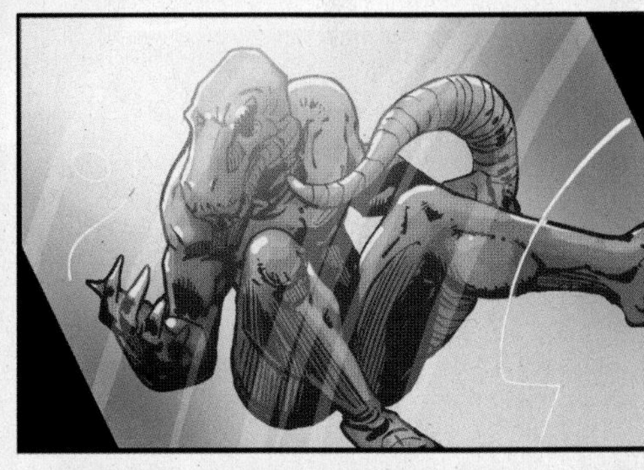

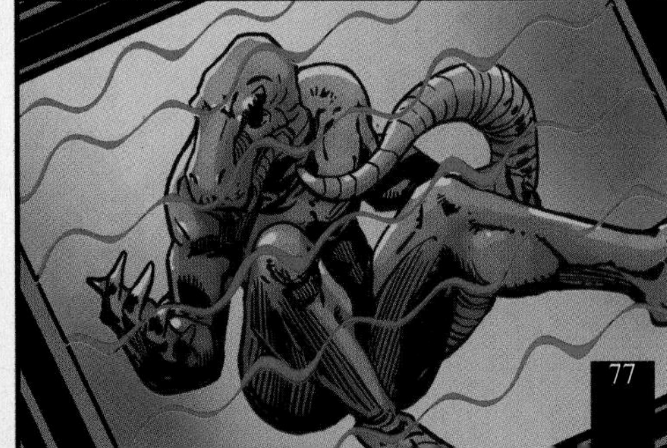

++FILE ERROR++
THAT CAN'T BE ALL. WHAT HAPPENED NEXT?
THE FILE APPEARS TO BE DAMAGED.
PLEASE, BUGGY. YOU HAVE TO FIX IT.
BUZZ BUZZZZZZ
NOW WE'LL NEVER KNOW WHAT HAPPENED.
CAN YOU AT LEAST DOWNLOAD THE FILES SO WE CAN ATTEMPT TO REPAIR THEM LATER?
BEEP BEEP BONG
FILES DOWNLOADING
5%

DOWNLOAD STOPPED AT 98%...

I GOT A **PRISONER** FOR YOU, MASTER ZALEX. I CAUGHT HIM MESSING AROUND WITH THE **COMPUTERS.**
IS THAT SO?

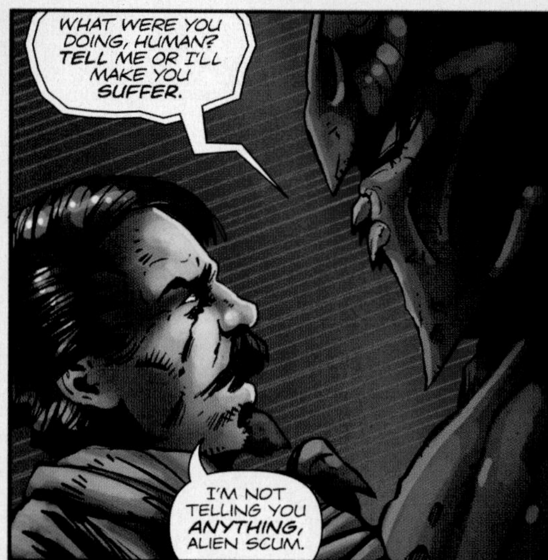
WHAT WERE YOU DOING, HUMAN? **TELL** ME OR I'LL MAKE YOU **SUFFER.**
I'M NOT TELLING YOU **ANYTHING,** ALIEN SCUM.

THERE WAS ANOTHER HUMAN, BUT IT GOT AWAY.

THEN FIND THIS "OTHER HUMAN"... AND **DESTROY** IT.
NO!
YOU **CAN'T.**

LOCK HIM UP. I'LL DEAL WITH HIM **LATER.**

GENETIC SCAN COMPLETE

THEN NOBODY CAN STAND IN MY WAY. AND THE GALAXY WILL BE MINE TO CONQUER!

WHERE ARE YOU TAKING ME?

MASTER ZALEX HAS A SPECIAL PLAN FOR YOU.

YOU WILL SOON BE ONE OF US.

AT LAST, MY BROTHER. WE WILL STAND SIDE-BY-SIDE AS MASTER ZALEX'S **GREATEST** WARRIORS. WE WILL BE **UNSTOPPABLE!**
I'LL **NEVER** JOIN YOU!
I'M AFRAID YOU HAVE NO **CHOICE**, REX!
WE'RE ON OUR **OWN**, BUGGY!
NOW WE HAVE TO **SAVE** STRIKE FORCE... AND MY **DAD**.
BEEP BEEP BUZZ

JURASSIC STRIKE FORCE 5

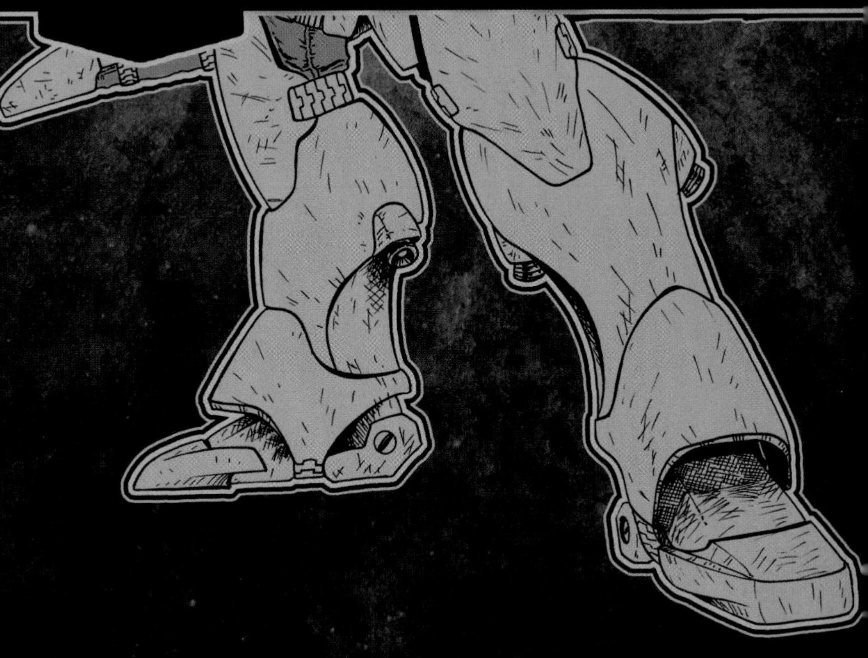

Chapter Four
WRITER NEO EDMUND ART JL GILES-RIVERA
COLORS JEFF BALKE LETTERS JIM CAMPBELL
CAIO CACAU

EXCAVATION SITE ALPHA -- REPTILIAN BASE.
KRRRRZZZ
KLANNG

WHERE YOU WANTS ME TO PUT THIS BOOM-BOOM?
BE CAREFUL WITH THAT MISSILE, YOU FOOL.
ONE SLIP AND YOU COULD DESTROY EVERYTHING FOR A HUNDRED MILES.

MEANWHILE, DEEP BENEATH THE BASE--

THINGS **COULDN'T** BE ANY **WORSE.**

CAPTURE THE HUMAN WE MUST.

REWARD US, MASTER ZALEX WILL.

MY DAD IS BEING HELD **HOSTAGE** BY **MUTANT DINOSAURS** AND NOW THEY'RE AFTER **ME.**

BEEP BEEP BUZZZZZZZ
TZAAK
TZAAK

YEAH, BUGGY! YOU UGLY LIZARD FACES ARE GOING TO **GET** IT NOW.

THE CARETAKER ANDROID.
WHY DOES IT **ATTACK** US?
TZAAK

BEEP BEEP BUZZZZZZZ

DESTROY IT, WE SHALL.
AFTER IT, YOU FOOL!

AWESOME!
NOW I JUST HAVE TO **RESCUE** STRIKE FORCE. AND THEN FIND MY **DAD**.

IT'S A GOOD THING THOSE REPTILIANS AREN'T HALF AS SMART AS THEY ARE BIG, OR I'D NEVER GET OUT OF HERE.
CHIK
AS TYLER WOULD SAY, MAJOR COOLNESS.
NOW I JUST NEED TO FIND TYLER AND FIGURE OUT HOW TO STOP A GANG OF MUTANT DINOSAURS THAT WANT TO TAKE OVER THE WORLD.

<GENETIC RESEQUENCING COMPOUND 71% COMPLETE>

I'LL ***NEVER*** JOIN YOUR EVIL FORCES, ZALEX.

WHEN MY GENETIC ALTERING SERUM IS **COMPLETE**, YOU WILL HAVE NO **CHOICE**...

IF THERE'S A CHANCE TO SAVE MY DAD, I'LL NEED **MAJOR** HELP.
NOW I JUST GOTTA FIGURE OUT HOW TO BUST OUT STRIKE FORCE BEFORE IT'S **TOO LATE**.
HEY, KID, YOU GOTTA GET US **OUT** OF HERE.
TELL ME SOMETHING I **DON'T** KNOW. ANY IDEA **HOW?**
THE CELL LOCK RELEASE IS ON THE FAR WALL.
Oh, NO! I'M GOING TO NEED A MAJOR **BOOST**!

FRIEND = FAVORED COMPANION

HEY! WAIT FOR ME!

THIS THING WEIGHS A TON. I GOTTA FIND SOMETHING ELSE.

HURRY UP, KID. THIS CAGE IS SO SMALL I'M GETTING A CRAMP IN MY TAIL.

HOLD ON TO YOUR DINO DRAWERS. I'M WORKING ON IT.

I CAN'T BELIEVE OUR FATE IS IN THE HANDS OF A FOOLISH CHILD.

WE'RE LOCKED IN CAGES AND THE KID IS RUNNING FREE, SO WHO'S THE FOOL, TANK?

IF HE DOESN'T GET US OUT BEFORE ZALEX FINISHES HIS SUPER WEAPON, IT WON'T MATTER.

WHOA.
THINGS HAVE GONE FROM BAD TO TOTALLY MESSED UP.

YOU HAVEN'T WON ***YET***, ZALEX.

Oh, NO! TOTAL **DOOMSDAY**.

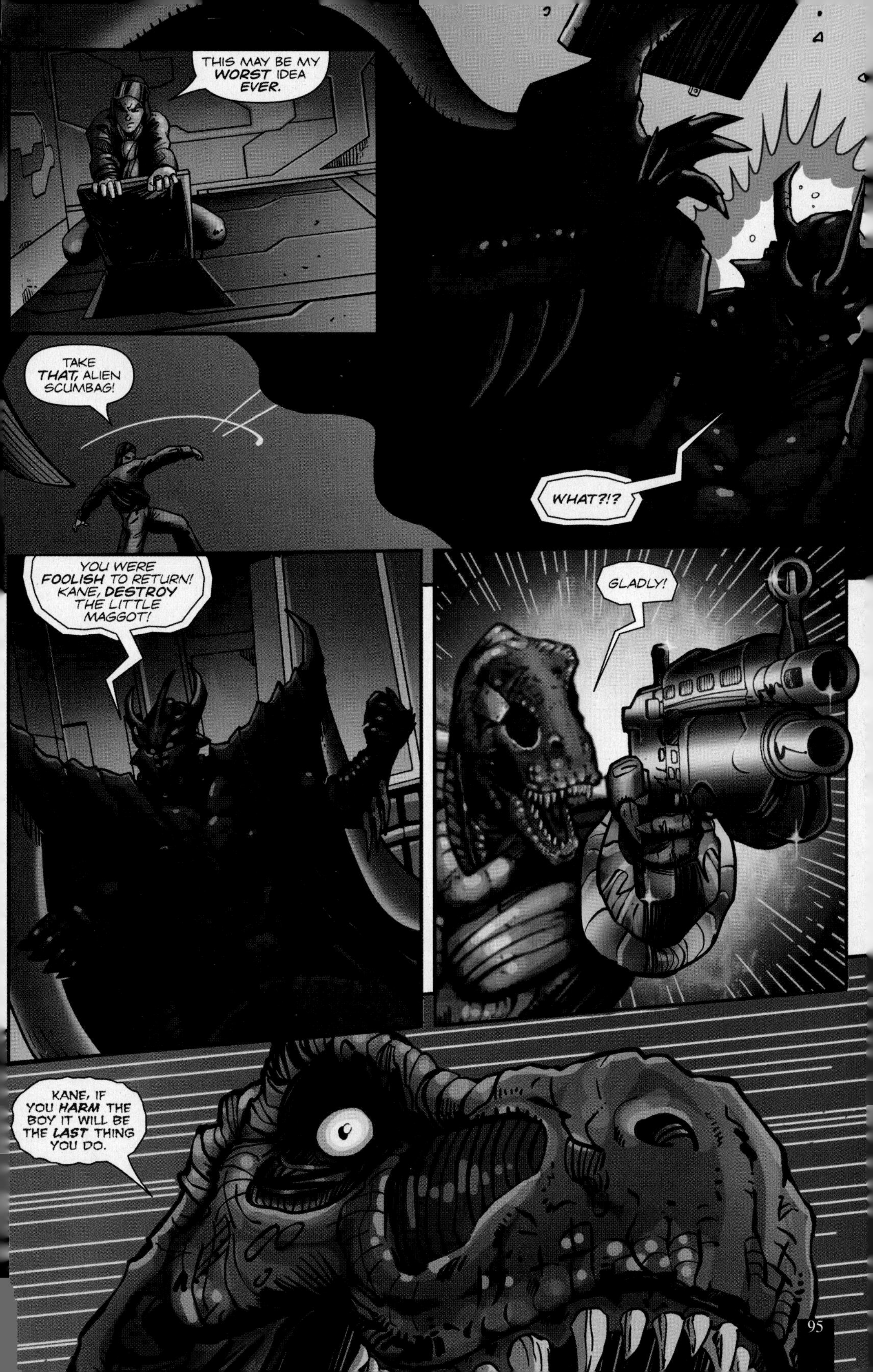
THIS MAY BE MY WORST IDEA EVER.
TAKE THAT, ALIEN SCUMBAG!
WHAT?!?
YOU WERE FOOLISH TO RETURN! KANE, DESTROY THE LITTLE MAGGOT!
GLADLY!
KANE, IF YOU HARM THE BOY IT WILL BE THE LAST THING YOU DO.

SHRAAK
YIKES!
FTOOM
KANE, YOU FOOL. YOU'VE DESTROYED OUR PRIMARY SCIENCE TERMINAL!
YOU GOTTA BE QUICKER THAN THAT!
I WILL MAKE YOU SUFFER FOR THAT, HUMAN!

HOW IS THIS HELPING US, KID?
HEY! I'M DOING THE BEST I CAN HERE.

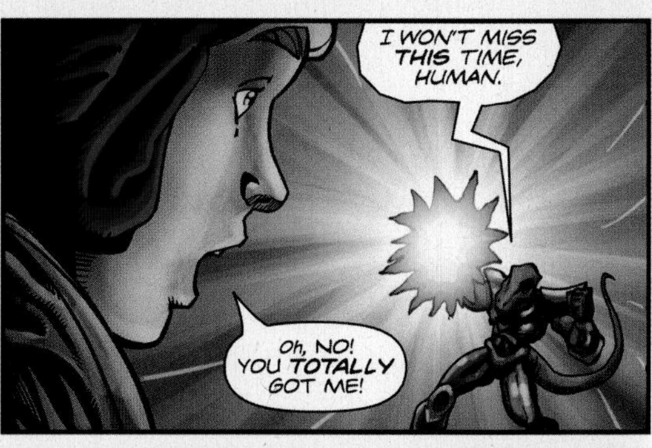
I WON'T MISS THIS TIME, HUMAN.
Oh, NO! YOU TOTALLY GOT ME!

NICE SHOOTING, SUCKER!
SHRAAAAKK

NOT BAD, KID!

NOOOOOO!

THANKS FOR THE BOOST!

NOW WE'RE GOING TO SEE SOME SERIOUS ACTION...

STRIKE FORCE,
ATTACK!

EMERGENCY IN THE SCIENCE LAB. STRIKE FORCE HAS ESCAPED.
WE GOTTA SAVE REX BEFORE THEY TURN HIM INTO A REPTILIAN.
TOO LATE, STRIKE FORCE.
STRIKE FORCE, YOU MUST GET OUT OF HERE. THAT'S AN ORDER.
STRIKE FORCE NEVER LEAVES A TEAMMATE BEHIND.
ARGHHHHH!
NOOOO!

STRIKE FORCE -- WE GOTTA SAVE REX BEFORE IT'S TOO LATE!

EASIER SAID THAN DONE, HUMAN.

PREVENT THEM FROM ESCAPING, WE MUST.

I TOLD YOU WE SHOULD HAVE DESTROYED THEM WHEN WE HAD THE CHANCE.
LOOKS LIKE WERE GONNA GET OUR CHANCE RIGHT NOW.

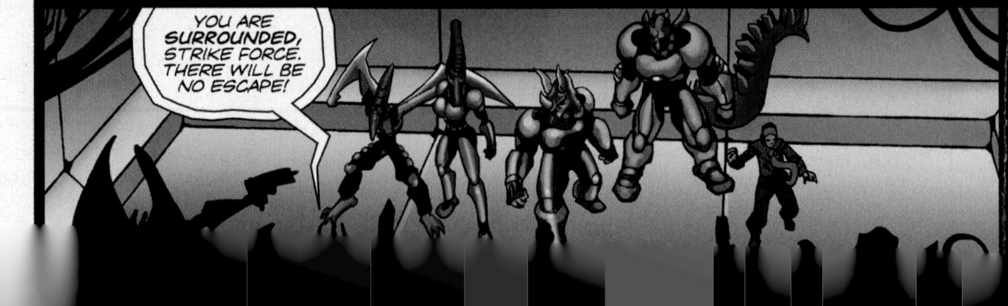
YOU ARE SURROUNDED, STRIKE FORCE. THERE WILL BE NO ESCAPE!

WHAT IS THAT THING DOING HERE?
BUZZZZZZ BUZZZZZZ
TZZAKK
TZAAK
TZAAK
TZZAKK
TZAAK
TZAAAK

BUZZZZZ BUZZZZZ
YOU ROCK, BUGGY! I'M SURE GLAD YOU'RE OUR FRIEND.

YOU WILL ALL BE DESTROYED FOR THIS INSOLENCE!
DIE, STRIKE FORCE!
KSHANGG
THOK
FWAM
AND NOW I SHALL FINISH WHAT I HAVE BEGUN!
KTHUD

NO! WHERE HAS THE SERUM GONE?

LOOKING FOR THIS?

SKAASH

CURSE YOU, HUMAN!

YOU MAY HAVE STOPPED ME FROM CONVERTING STRIKE FORCE, BUT YOU WILL NOT LIVE TO TELL THE TALE.

<SELF-DESTRUCT SEQUENCE ACTIVATED>
UH-OH! WE'VE GOT A MAJOR SITUATION HERE!

STRIKE FORCE. **FORGET** ME! SAVE **YOURSELVES**.

WE'RE NOT LEAVING WITHOUT YOU, REX.

WE ONLY HAVE **SECONDS** BEFORE THE ENTIRE PLACE WILL BE **DESTROYED**.

WE CAN'T LEAVE WITHOUT MY **DAD**.

TYLER. **OVER HERE!**

TYLER, WHERE HAVE YOU **BEEN?** I WAS **VERY** CONCERNED.

CHILL **OUT**, DAD. I **TOTALLY** HAD IT UNDER **CONTROL**.

Oh, NO! THE REPTILIANS ARE TOTALLY GETTING AWAY.
GOODBYE, STRIKE FORCE. I AM OFF TO MEET THE LEADERS OF THIS WORLD AND UNLEASH MY ULTIMATE WEAPON!

JURASSIC STRIKE FORCE 5

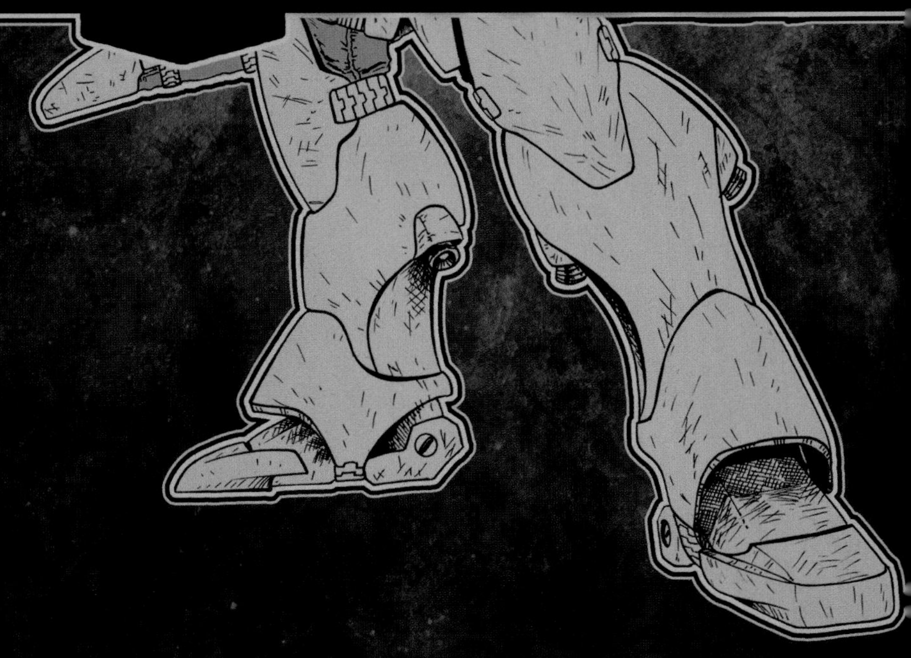

Chapter Five
WRITER NEO EDMUND ART RYAN HOWE & ARMANDO RILLO
COLORS JEFF BALKE LETTERS JIM CAMPBELL

U.S. SUBMARINE BASE, ANTARCTICA--

GIVE ME *ONE* REASON WHY WE SHOULDN'T BLAST YOU MUTANT FREAKS TO *BITS* RIGHT HERE AND NOW!

WASHINGTON, DC--
KABOOM
MY SPINOSAURUS IS INVINCIBLE!

THE WHITE HOUSE, OVAL OFFICE--
MISTER PRESIDENT, OUR FORCES DON'T STAND A CHANCE AGAINST THESE MUTANT DINOSAURS.
THEIR ALIEN LEADER, ZALEX, DEMANDS OUR SURRENDER OR HE'LL REDUCE THE CITY TO ASHES.

AMERICANS NEVER SURRENDER!
WE'LL FIGHT THESE FREAKS TO THE BITTER END.

IT MAY COME TO THAT, SIR. THEY'VE SEIZED SEVERAL OF OUR NUCLEAR WEAPONS.

THEN WE'RE GOING TO NEED A MIRACLE. TELL ME OUR OPTIONS.

WE HAVE ONLY ONE. I DON'T THINK YOU'RE GOING TO LIKE IT.

US AIR FORCE

THIS IS TAKING FOREVER. ARE WE THERE YET?

LISTEN UP, ROCK BRAINS. WE LAND IN DC IN FOURTEEN MINUTES. THE REPTILIAN ATTACK IS ALREADY UNDERWAY AND OUR FORCES ARE TAKING A POUNDING.

WHEN WE ARRIVE, I NEED YOUR TROOPS TO PULL OUT. LET US HANDLE ZALEX.
REX, I REFUSE TO PUT THE SECURITY OF OUR NATION IN THE HANDS OF A BUNCH OF MUTANTS.

GENERAL, YOU MAY NOT HAVE A CHOICE.

TRUST ME, YOU DON'T WANT TO BE NEARBY WHEN I UNLEASH MY RHINO BLASTER.

LET'S JUST HOPE IT WILL PENETRATE THE ARMOR OF THAT SPINOSAURUS...
OR THE EARTH IS DOOMED.

WHOA!
I KNOW WHAT'S AT THE TOP OF MY CHRISTMAS LIST.

NO WAY! A BATTLE TECH HEADS-UP CONTROL SYSTEM.

A GUY COULD KICK SOME MAJOR REPTILIAN TAIL IN THIS THING.

HEY, KID! GET OUT OF THAT EXO-MECH PROTOTYPE.
IT TAKES HUNDREDS OF TRAINING HOURS TO PILOT THAT RIG.
NOT EVEN. I'VE PLAYED VIDEO GAMES WITH TOUGHER CONTROL SETUPS.
WELL, HELLO! DO I SMELL STRIKE FORCE?

FTOOM

THE ENGINES ARE DONE FOR.
WE'RE GOING DOWN!

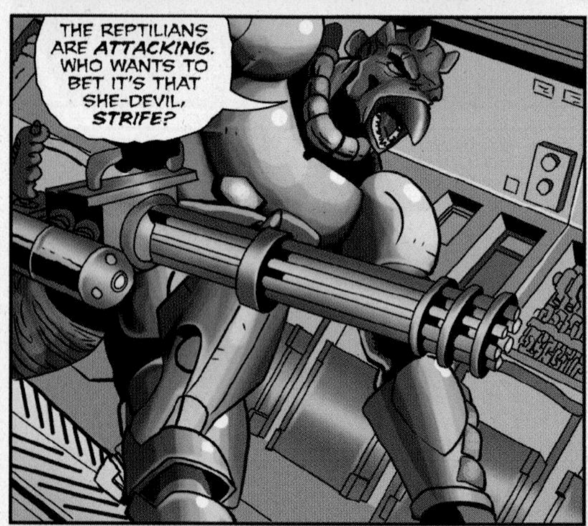
THE REPTILIANS ARE ATTACKING. WHO WANTS TO BET IT'S THAT SHE-DEVIL, STRIFE?

YOU TWO STAY CLOSE. I'LL PROTECT YOU!
I TOLD YOU GUYS WE SHOULD NEVER FLY COACH.

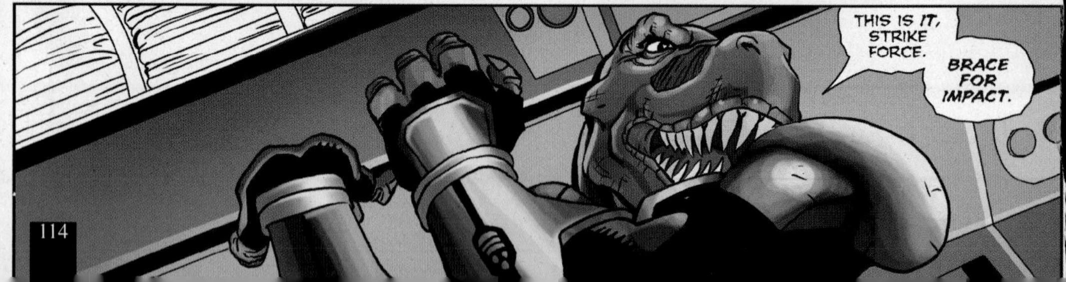
THIS IS IT, STRIKE FORCE.
BRACE FOR IMPACT.

KRAAASH

SEE YOU AROUND, STRIKE FORCE!

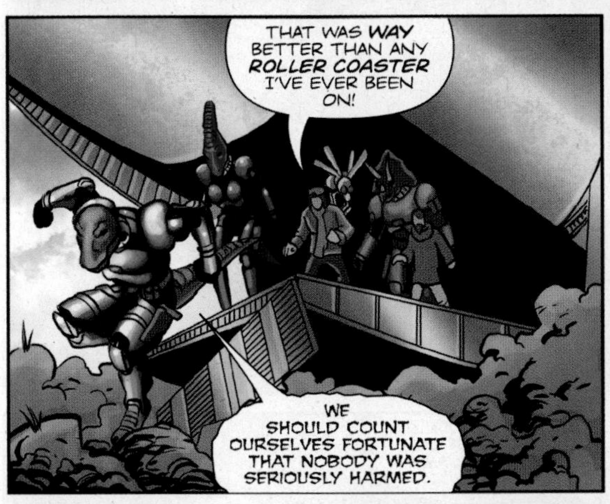
THAT WAS WAY BETTER THAN ANY ROLLER COASTER I'VE EVER BEEN ON!
WE SHOULD COUNT OURSELVES FORTUNATE THAT NOBODY WAS SERIOUSLY HARMED.

SPEAK FOR YOURSELF, REX. MY TAIL MAY NEVER BE THE SAME!

ELIMINATE STRIKE FORCE, WE SHALL!
REWARD US, MASTER ZALEX WILL.

AHHHHH!!

REX! NOOO!

LOOK OUT! IT'S THE FREAK TWINS, RAZOR AND TALON.
LET'S MAKE 'EM HISTORY!

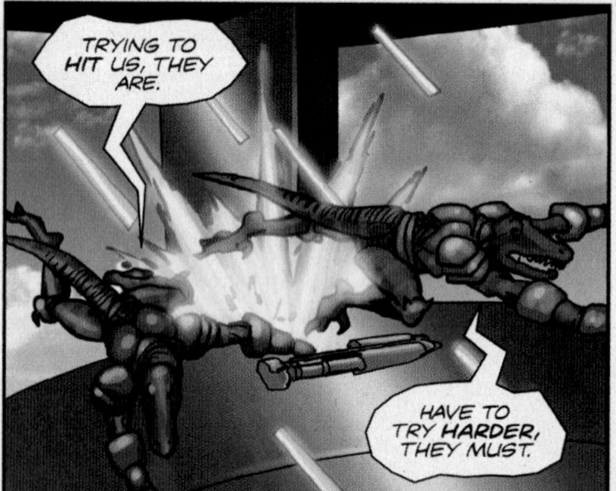
TRYING TO HIT US, THEY ARE.
HAVE TO TRY HARDER, THEY MUST.

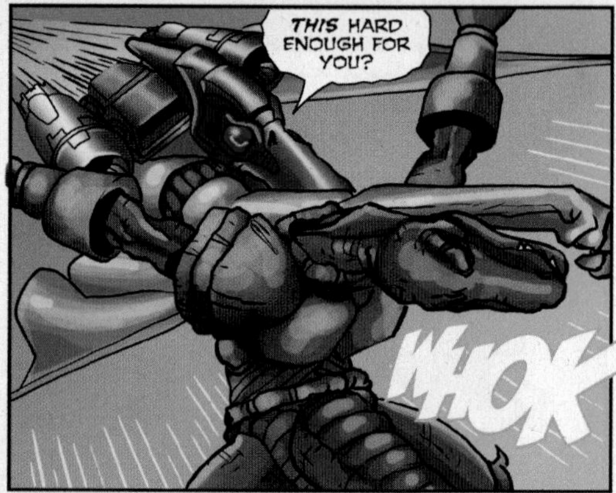
THIS HARD ENOUGH FOR YOU?
WHOK

WHUDD
WE CAN TRY HARDER IF YOU WANT US TO.

IF MASTER ZALEX LEARNS OF OUR FAILURE, PUNISH US HE WILL.
THEN FLEE FROM HERE, WE MUST.

RAAAAAHHH

MAJOR BAD NEWS. MY RHINO BLASTER DIDN'T EVEN MAKE THAT SPINOSAURUS *FLINCH*.

THE MAJOR *GOOD* NEWS IS THAT YOU DIDN'T BLOW THE *NUKE*. LOOK!

ANY *OTHER* GREAT IDEAS, KID?
DON'T LOOK AT ME. REX PUT *YOU* IN CHARGE.

I HAVE AN IDEA, STRIKE FORCE!
YOU ALL DIE!

GAATT
TATTTTT
TAAATTTTT

ARGHHGHHHH!

SHUT IT DOWN, SPIKE. YOU'LL DESTROY US ALL!

WHAT IS IT WITH YOU ALIEN OVERLORDS ALWAYS WANTING TO RULE THE GALAXY?

DAD, PLEASE TELL ME REX IS GOING TO BE OKAY.
IT'S HARD TO SAY, TYLER. I'M NOT A DINO DOCTOR.
WE MUST GET YOU MEDICAL ATTENTION.
NO TIME, SARAL. ZALEX AND THE REPTILIANS MUST BE STOPPED.
YOU'RE IN NO CONDITION FOR A FIGHT, OLD FRIEND.
YOU MAY BE RIGHT, TANK. YOU LEAD THE TEAM.
I'LL JOIN THE FIGHT AS SOON AS I RECOVER.
AH-YEAH! TIME FOR SOME DINO-SIZE BATTLE ACTION.
SORRY. NO KIDS ALLOWED IN THIS FIGHT.
BEFORE THIS FIGHT IS OVER, YOU'RE GONNA NEED MY HELP TO SAVE THE DAY. YOU'LL SEE!
HA! HOW COULD A SCRAWNY RUNT LIKE YOU EVER HELP US?
LOCK AND LOAD, STRIKE FORCE.
WE'RE GOING IN!

ARGHHH!

UMPHHHH!

OH, NO!

I THINK WE'RE IN *SERIOUS* TROUBLE!

I'M NOT DEAD YET, KANE.

YOU WILL BE SOON ENOUGH, MY FOOLISH BROTHER.
THEN LET THIS BE OUR FINAL BATTLE.

SHZANNG

SNAPP

RAHHHHH!

ARGHHHH!

RARRRRR!

YOU'RE DEFEATED, KANE.

REX, I SEE THAT **YOU** ARE THE STRONGER BROTHER. IT IS A PITY I MUST NOW **DESTROY** YOU!

I'VE WAITED A ***LONG*** TIME TO FACE YOU, ZALEX.

ARRHHHH!

KRAK

HAHAHAHAHAHA! I'VE CONQUERED HUNDREDS OF WORLDS.
I WILL NEVER BE DEFEATED BY SUCH A FUTILE ATTACK!

DIE, REX!

AAAHHHHH!
KZAAKKK

HANG ON, REX! I'M COMING!

SARAL! NOOOOO!

KZAAKKK

FOOLISH GIRL! SUCH MISGUIDED COMPASSION WILL ONLY BRING YOUR DESTRUCTION.
NOW YOU WILL DIE TOGETHER.

WHAT?!
SHRAAK

GUYS, DIDN'T I SAY YOU WOULD NEED MY HELP TO SAVE THE DAY?
NOW, LET'S SEE WHAT THIS THING CAN REALLY DO.

FIRE FULL MELEE PAYLOAD!

FTOOM

SURRENDER, ZALEX. DON'T MAKE ME DESTROY YOU!

NEVER!
WHOK

ENJOY YOUR VICTORY, STRIKE FORCE. FOR HOWEVER LONG YOU CAN.

REPTILIANS, IT IS TIME TO MAKE OUR DEPARTURE.
WHAT ABOUT THE SPINOSAURUS?

LET STRIKE FORCE DEAL WITH IT!

DID THEY JUST ESCAPE THROUGH A TEMPORAL VORTEX?
IT SEEMS ZALEX HAS LEARNED SOME NEW TRICKS.
FORGET THEM. WE GOTTA STOP THAT BOMB.

THE CONTROL PANEL IS HISTORY. THERE'S NO WAY IT CAN BE DISARMED!
THEN WE HAVE TO GET IT AS FAR FROM HERE AS POSSIBLE.
BOOMER, GIVE ME YOUR ROCKET PACK.
NOT A CHANCE, REX. THESE OLD JETS WON'T FLY HIGH ENOUGH.
BOOMER IS RIGHT. YOU'D HAVE TO GET THE BOMB ABOVE THE EARTH'S ATMOSPHERE TO AVOID THE RADIOACTIVE FALLOUT.
THEN I NEED TO FIND A WAY TO FLY REALLY HIGH, REALLY FAST.
IF YOU ROCK BRAINS NEED A RIDE INTO THE WILD BLUE YONDER, ALL YOU HAVE TO DO IS ASK!
YOUR FRIENDLY NEIGHBORHOOD U.S. AIR FORCE KNOWS ALL ABOUT AIMING HIGH.

THIS MAY BE MY WORST IDEA IN A HUNDRED MILLION YEARS.
0:59
GETTING HARD TO BREATHE UP HERE.
END OF THE ROAD!
0:11
RAGHHHHHH!
0:01

YOU WERE MY HERO, REX. I'LL NEVER FORGET YOU!
I KNOW HOW YOU FEEL, KID. REX WAS MY HERO, TOO.
WAIT. I SEE SOMETHING.
IT'S REX! HE'S TOTALLY OUT OF CONTROL. WE HAVE TO DO SOMETHING!
JETS DON'T FAIL ME NOW!
GOT YOU!
YOU'RE A LOT HEAVIER THAN YOU LOOK, OLD FRIEND.
THEY'RE GOING TO CRASH!
SPLASSH

THANKS FOR THE SAVE.
DON'T MENTION IT, REX.
REX, YOU TOTALLY SAVED THE WORLD!
STRIKE FORCE. WE'VE WON A GREAT VICTORY TODAY AGAINST ZALEX, BUT THE WAR HAS ONLY BEGUN.
WHEN THE REPTILIANS TURN UP AGAIN, WE'LL BE READY TO TAKE THEM DOWN.
AND I'LL BE HERE TO HELP YOU SAVE THE DAY!
I HAVE A FEELING THE MILITARY IS GOING TO WANT THAT EXO-MECH BACK.
MAJOR BUMMER!
DON'T WORRY, KID. I'LL BUILD YOU A NEW ONE, EVEN BETTER THAN THAT HUNK OF JUNK!
YOU ROCK, TANK!

I THINK YOU GUYS NEED A COOLER NAME.
HOW ABOUT JURASSIC STRIKE FORCE 5!
NOW YOU'RE TALKING, KID!
VERY WELL. THEN FROM THIS DAY ON, THAT IS HOW WE SHALL BE KNOWN IN OUR QUEST TO SAVE THE EARTH FROM ZALEX AND HIS EVIL REPTILIANS.
HEY, GUYS. ANYBODY KNOW WHAT HAPPENED TO THE SPINOSAURUS?
THE END...FOR NOW.